AF483769

GIRLS' LUNCH

A New Orleans Memoir

by

Monica L. Monica

ISBN: 979-8-8690-1571-6

Illustrations and book cover art by Michael Verrett

Azalea

Considered the most abundant flower for Louisiana landscaping bushes of the multicolored Azalea were imported over 200 years ago. Jackson Square in New Orleans is but one of the places to see the springtime renewal of purple, pink, fuchsia, and white blooms.

TO:

MY BELOVED PARENTS, LOU AND GINNY
MONICA, WHO STARTED MY STORY IN
NEW ORLEANS WHILE AT TULANE
UNIVERSITY.

MY HUSBAND, DAN, AND MY CHILDREN,
DANIELLE AND LISA, WHO CONTINUED
THE STORY.

TABLE OF CONTESTS

Mississippi Riverboat

In 1811 the *New Orleans*, became the first riverboat to ply the waters of the Mississippi River. Its voyage began at Pittsburgh, on the Ohio Rivers and concluded to its destination at New Orleans. Though glamorous, the technology of the day had trouble keeping pace with the desires of its inventor as an average of one boat a week exploded due to poor construction.

CHAPTER ONE

It was strange, preparing to have lunch with the girls

after twenty-five years. We were finally getting back together

again.

"Ah, the girls' lunch!" I said with glee.

Our lunches often received prime press in the social

columns and were maligned and desired by many socialites

in New Orleans who vied for invitations. We became the

topic of many cocktail parties around town, having more fun

along the way than legally allowed.

Our lunch was finally going to happen again. I could

almost taste the salty, succulent oysters and hear the girls'

laughter. We were returning to the Sazerac Restaurant

where it all began, and the anticipation made me giddy and

carefree.

"Laissez les bon temps rouler! " I said.

On an anniversary trip to New Orleans with my husband, I reached out to the girls. We dined at Tommy's Cuisine on Tchoupitoulas Street, a favorite restaurant, savoring mussels with linguini, shrimp corn chowder, and spaghetti and meatballs while sitting in our special corner table under a photo of ourselves on the wall. I knew we were well-known because of that photo.

Sergio, our waiter and friend, always took control of the menu, because he knew our favorite dishes by heart. When he served my husband and me, he asked, "How are your lady friends?" He served our girls' lunch many times.

I realized I didn't know the answer. I corresponded with the girls over the years through holiday and birthday cards, but there was no meaningful communication.

That fact prompted a phone call to each to them and an invitation to meet again for lunch.

"I'll be in New Orleans in a few months for a meeting," I explained. "Let's get together for lunch."

Each of them accepted.

Our group consisted of six gorgeous, dynamic, fearless women in their thirties who met through social and professional networks in New Orleans. What brought each of us to New Orleans varied, from local family roots to marriage, or to work-related moves. We all shared a deep love of life, food, good times, and wanting to have it all. We were hungry for the best in all aspects of life, but happily, we weren't ruthless in our methods of attaining our goals. We weren't shy, either. Along the way were plenty of hardships in the pursuit of our dreams. We may have gotten more than we bargained for, but that was part of our pact with life.

Each month, one of us chose a fabulous New Orleans restaurant and planned the luncheon. Some went overboard with extraordinary decorations, flowers, and favors, especially with theme luncheons at Halloween or

Christmas. Once for a birthday lunch, the Olympia Brass

Band played us into the restaurant, as we walked in a line

behind them.

Sometimes, we lunched in the common dining

rooms, sharing space with locals and tourists. Other times,

we had a private kitchen set up or a room to ourselves. I

especially enjoyed dining at the chef's table in the restaurant

kitchen amidst the frantic activity and amazing smells.

Seated there in the middle of the action, I felt connected to

the heart of the restaurant, which added a little lagniappe to

the entire experience. A few times, we had lunch on yachts

with famous chefs like Emeril Lagasse catering to our

culinary needs.

In the end, though, the venues were just the

backdrop to the dram and excitement generated by our

conversation.

I always remembered the first lunch at the Sazerac

Room in the Fairmont Hotel. We started at noon and

finished around five o'clock. Everyone in the room knew we were there thanks to our raucous laughter. Some of the grand dames of New Orleans sent scowls and disapproving head shakes our way, but mostly, the customers strained to overhear us. A group of businessmen seated at the next table spent more time eavesdropping and checking us out than discussing their company financial reports.

At the end of their lunch, one of the distinguished corporate heads sauntered over to our table and asked, "Where's the next lunch? We'd like to book the table beside yours."

So it began, the infamous girls' lunches with loud laughter that made all around us envious. Some restaurants offered private dining venues just to contain our loud, bawdy camaraderie. One restaurant asked us not to return. Most felt privileged to have the press and notoriety our group generated.

So much had happened since that first lunch at the

Fairmont. I wondered how we would react to each other now that we were in our fifties.

Will that youthful woman in each of us emerge again to emit raucous laughter, or instead, will there be a more-mature, contemplative woman in her place? I asked myself.

I hoped we had time for some banal banter over Kir Royales, then a gradual transition to the topics of our lives. We all needed to be brought up-to-date on what happened to each of us, although I wasn't sure I wanted to know the specific details. Sometimes it was nice to be ignorant of the present and live in the past. I discovered as I grew older that change was more difficult to accept, at least for me.

Ten years earlier, I moved from New Orleans to Beaver Creek, Colorado, a very big change for me. Mountain climate and lifestyle were a far cry from living in the Deep South. My husband and I owned twenty acres nestled against the mountains outside Beaver Creek. We rode horses, went whitewater rafting, and enjoyed skiing.

We enjoyed our active lifestyle. Our grandchildren learned to ski on Hay Meadows in Beaver Creek. During fall and winter breaks from school, they visited to enjoy life in the High Country. The loved telling spooky stories around the campfire while making s'mores. Life was nearly perfect.

Although there were some changes after Katrina, New Orleans appeared much the same to me. One thing was certain—the weather in the Big Easy was the same, steamy and muggy in August. Dealing with the weather in New Orleans was like learning to ride a bicycle—a person never forgot. Living there, you understood you lived in a bowl below sea level, and any deluge of rain could cause massive flooding. The city flooded during Katrina not so much due to the hurricane but due to the substandard construction of the levees that broke. The pumps in the pumping stations dated back to the 1900s. Everyone agreed afterward that the equipment needed upgrades and replacement.

I stayed at the Pontchartrain Hotel on St. Charles Avenue, a beautiful old building whose history included patrons such as Liz Taylor, Richard Burton, presidents, and foreign dignitaries. I loved the hotel for many reasons, not the least of which was their signature dessert called Mile-High Pie. When living in New Orleans, I devoured many slices of that gooey, decadent dessert.

As I walked outside my hotel to grab a cab, my clothes were already sticking to my skin. I wanted my new Prada outfit to look chic, not like something I picked up at the local Goodwill. I was counting on the group to react to how fabulous I looked due to my weight loss. Thankfully, the cab's AC was functioning, and we drove down the Avenue.

St. Charles Avenue is one of the world's most-beautiful streets, with 100-year-old oaks sending branches above the trolley tracks to embrace each other. The clanking of the trolley cars under those branches mixed with the visual beauty of the homes made it an iconic location.

Some of the homes there were plantation estates before the

Civil War, with huge stretches of land extending to the

Mississippi. The grand-pillared Greek-Revival mansions,

with wraparound porches, represented the grandeur of the

old South. I could easily imagine women in giant hoop

skirts fanning themselves on the porch while being served

lemonade. It felt as if Scarlet O'Hara would appear any

minute. New Orleans was ripe with history, albeit some very

hard to defend or stomach, including the slave trade. I

always felt like I traveled back in time when I visited the "city

that care forgot."

I once lived in an old Victorian mansion in the

Garden District, surrounded by the majesty of those

magnificent old oaks. The mansion was affordable only due

to my husband's success in selling a program patent for data

security. My journey to that old home began as students,

when we went through the Irish Channel and lived in a

shotgun apartment, complete with roaches, that cost only

$175 a month. The name shotgun came from the fact that if

someone fired a shotgun from the front room, it would go

straight through the apartment to the back room.

Our furnishings consisted of a Sear's mattress on the

floor, a table made from a street sign perched on bricks,

which doubled as a dining and coffee table, and an old

wingback chair. We spent many Saturday mornings

drinking *café au lait* and reading the newspaper in the shared

portico with our neighbors.

I told myself that one day, I would miss the

apartment and my life there. I thought I'd welcome leaving

behind the days of a poor medical intern married to a grad

student, but I was wrong. I quickly learned that money and

success didn't guarantee peace and happiness. As life got

better, it often became more complicated.

The times spent in the Garden District were fun,

with St. Patrick's Day parades, bike rides to Audubon Park

and the French quarter, and crawfish boils in the shared

patio. Our neighbors were a diverse group, with a stock

broker living overhead whose aggressive financial moves

eventually landed him in Federal prison; a restaurateur in

the next apartment, whose love of rich food and long hours

killed him with a heart attack; and a French seamstress in the

next building who introduced me to French pastries and

Chanel couture. Across the street lived a madam who

catered to the wealthy businessmen of New Orleans. She

had a water-tight insurance policy, namely the Chief of

Police, who was a client. Her business thrived. I later

learned she inherited money from a former client and

retired to live in the Bahamas. She certainly did all right for

herself.

We drove around Lee Circle, where the statue of

Robert E. Lee stood proudly on a pedestal facing north,

because the story went that he would never turn his back on

the South.

"They're going to move the General," the cabbie said, "because he represents the racist days of the South."

I felt conflicted about politics changing the outcome of history, but I didn't speak. Instead, I checked my makeup in the mirror and discovered the AC in the cab hadn't prevented my makeup from running down my cheeks until I looked like a clown. I applied lip gel, blotted my cheeks with a tissue, and hoped for the best.

Finally, we reached the front of the Roosevelt where it all began. A uniformed bellman opened the door and said, "Welcome to the Fairmont."

As I climbed the steps, I felt as if I went back in time. I remembered the first photos of our group taken on those steps. All the girls were young, lovely, ambitious, and smart. What women could take their places?

I strolled into the beautiful lobby with its magnificent mosaic floor, passed the early 1900s antique clock, and headed to the Sazerac Restaurant. The *maître d'* pretended to remember me and said, "So glad to have you back."

I remembered the plush velvet banquettes and waiters dashing from table to table, delivering martinis to well-dressed ladies. I passed the golden telephone on the stand, waiting to be taken to some mover and shaker's table.

Finally, I saw our table. In true Italian style, the girls sat facing the room. Terry nursed a whiskey sour and sat beside Jennifer and Adrien, who were in deep conversation. Courtney sat at the opposite end and scrutinized the others. I missed seeing Kathy's face, but she died twenty years earlier. Somehow, I felt she was there in spirit, saying, and "Let the games begin!"

As I made my final approach to the table, I reflected on each girl's life.

# French Quarter

Translation *'Old Quarter'*, it is oldest neighborhood in New Orleans. With narrow streets radiating from the river, one is transported to the late 1700's and early 1800's with architect representing French, Spanish, and Caribbean cultures. Of particular note are ornate cast iron 'galleries' and French balconies.

CHAPTER TWO

Terry

Terry was the one of us who truly landed on her feet. She was born in New Orleans, the product of two schoolteachers. She was quite a looker, and all the boys wanted to date her. Her looks were deceiving, though. Under those lustrous golden locks was a brilliant mind. She set her eye on something grander than her modest lifestyle. Attending public schools, she earned a scholarship to Tulane University, where she majored in chemistry and eventually earned her PhD, graduating *cum laude*. Her mantra was, "If you're going to do something, do it well." She stayed true to that motto in everything she accomplished.

Her first marriage was to a prominent man from New Orleans, named Stanley Adams, whose family owned one of the largest local coffee and food companies. His family made him attend school at Tulane before inheriting the reins of the company. When the two met at a fraternity mixer, it was love at first sight. Marrying after graduation, they settled into a beautiful home on St. Charles Avenue decorated with fine antiques and expensive artwork. Everyone campaigned to receive an invite to one of their extravagant parties. Their attendance at social occasions was much desired.

Around their tenth wedding anniversary, Stan became unexpectedly ill. He was diagnosed with pancreatic cancer, which is almost always a death sentence. Terry was devastated. Her biggest regret was that she and Stan had no children.

I met Terry at an Odyssey Ball fundraiser. She was gorgeous, without a blemish or a line on her porcelain skin.

She had cosmetic surgery at a young age and had multiple

body parts lifted and tightened. Not wanting to stay at home

and host teas, she started her own line of cosmetics and

facial creams that sold on popular home-shopping networks.

She actually made her chemistry degree pay off with her

company called Flawless and launched an organic-based spa

salon that catered to young, Junior League women while also

serving the grand dames of New Orleans.

Due to her personality and business acumen, her

business flourished. A spa date with Terry was as much a

social affair as a beauty appointment.

She was invited to all the right parties. Her sense of

humor trumped her beauty, and she could insult someone

with a one-line zinger and still make the person feel like it

was an offhanded compliment. Her wit, style, and smarts

were hard to match. I loved watching her work the room at

an event. All eyes were on her, and she knew it. She glided

over the floor, playing with people like a cat playing with

balls of yarn. She knew everyone's dirty little secrets, and no one dared cross or disappoint her if she knew what was best.

I always remembered the story after her intervention in a high-profile cheating scandal. It was during the Governor's annual Mardi Gras party when she sashayed up to a prominent lawyer, pulled him aside, and whispered sweetly, "Your mistress, Debra, is a wonderful girl and a regular at my salon. You certainly love dressing in ladies' black lingerie."

He turned pale and choked on his martini.

"You may want to reconsider where your loyalties lie and return home to your wife and children," Terry added.

He was so mortified about being discovered, he never strayed again. He knew Terry's powerful connections could make his successful life evaporate overnight. The mistress was upset about the loss of her luxurious lifestyle, so Terry fixed that problem by introducing her to a seventy-two-year-old Texas oil man. He wanted a beautiful woman

to squire around, and she was well-supported in return.
Each got what he or she wanted.

Terry loved solving problems.

When Terry organized a girls' lunch, it was quite an event. She always chose either Antoine's or Arnaud's Restaurant in the French Quarter. She had a jazz trio play in the corner during cocktails while *pomme du soufflé* potatoes and other small plates were passed around to enjoy. Then all the girls were ushered into a private dining room with the table set in exquisite china and crystal specially ordered, candelabras ablaze, and pink peony flower arrangements scattered throughout the room. Terry had the chef prepare most of the entrées, which were placed on the center of the table family style for each guest to sample.

The meal was capped off by a giant baked Alaska, accompanied by chilled champagne. We ended the lunch by singing loudly, *Do You Know What It Means to Miss New Orleans?* accompanied by a pianist.

Terry's second marriage was to an advertising genius named Mark Reynolds. He was a forty-five-year-old triathlon athlete who ran a global marketing agency that specialized in taking small companies and launching them to national prominence. She employed his firm to do the same for her business, and they sat for hours, strategizing and planning the campaign for Flawless, Inc. Terry's business sense meshed well with Mark's, and soon, they were engaged in more than just business.

Once, after a long strategy session, Mark proposed, and she gladly accepted. Soon, Flawless, Inc. rose to number one among its competitors. Terry made the Forbes list of the richest young women entrepreneurs. Her gorgeous face was displayed on many business publications.

Mark lived well. He owned a Gulfstream jet kept on standby to fly him to any of his residential properties or business meetings. He had a penthouse in Central Park West and a gorgeous home in the Hollywood Hills overlooking all of Los Angeles. Besides homes in the States,

he owned a Caribbean island in which he invested twenty

million dollars to create a tropical paradise for much-needed

fun and relaxation. On that island, with the sun shining and

tropical breezes blowing, Terry became Mrs. Mark Reynolds

in a simple ceremony with just the two of them—no fanfare

or long line of guests. They became a formidable, single

unit, ready to set the world on fire.

Before marrying Terry, Mark went through a terrible

divorce and was looking for a woman who enjoyed traveling,

working, and experiencing life without putting too many

demands on his time. Terry found those rules easy to

follow, because she was busy with her own company and

projects. After marriage, she jetted around, but she

managed to return to New Orleans for our lunches, looking

like a young, excited schoolgirl dying to share the latest

events in her life. She was wealthy beyond her dreams, but

more importantly, she was very happy. She felt nothing

would ever derail her perfect life.

No one knew that Mark had a double life as a bisexual who loved young men. Unfortunately, one of them turned out to be a minor, and he was the son of a prominent politician. The story hit the LA newspapers like wildfire. The young man's parents sued Mark for sexual assault on a minor.

Mark's career crashed, as did his marriage to Terry. Feeling betrayed, she moved back to New Orleans. She kept to herself a lot, creating the impression she was concentrating on running her business. We didn't see much of her. She withdrew from all contact. Only much later did I discover she was addicted to Valium and pain pills. It took her a long time, but she emerged from her addiction and tried to regain control of her life. She had been such a *tour de force* and so in control of everything, it was hard to believe she succumbed to addiction and spent most of her days in a fetal position on her couch. Clearly, no one was immune to life's challenges and difficulties. We just thought

we were.

Six months after checking into a rehabilitation

center, Terry called to invite me to spend a week wit her in

her condo on Seven Mile Beach on Grand Cayman Island, a

beautiful, British-owned island approximately four miles

wide by twenty-two long, surrounded by the Cayman

Trench.

Since that was one of my favorite destinations on the

planet, I jumped at the chance. We spent lazy days in the

sun, took long walks on the beach, went snorkeling, and

spent wonderful evenings dining on gourmet cuisine

prepared by her private chef and drinking fine wines. The

time spent in Grand Cayman with her was very special. She

shared her feelings with me and exhibited a vulnerability I

hadn't previously experienced in our relationship.

Terry seemed truly rejuvenated and threw herself

into her work. Once again, she had a sparkle in her eye and determination in her step. She developed several new

cosmetic products and controlled all aspects of their

development and launch. Her infomercials were all over the

TV. She traveled so much; there was rarely any time to get

together except for our lunches.

Finally, she withdrew from those, too, and I looked

forward to seeing her the most, wondering how her life had

worked out.

Historic Gallier Hall
545 St Charles Avenue

(1845 –1853) an extraordinary example of Greek Revival architecture the building originally served as city hall. It is the greatest example of designer James Gallier and designated as a National Historical Landmark. Located across from Lafayette Park, the building remains a vibrant part of the city with its three large ballrooms and other functions.

CHAPTER THREE

Jennifer

Jennifer was the "famous" girl in the group. Her

sapphire-blue eyes and long blonde hair defined her

Californian roots. She moved from Los Angeles to New

York City at the age of three, the daughter of very talented

parents. Robert was a famous Broadway director

responsible for many Tony Award-winning hits. Louise was

a Grammy Award-winning jazz singer from New Orleans

who performed at the Carlyle. She was called the female

version of Bobby Short. Since she grew up in such an

environment, show business was a key part of Jen's DNA.

She caught the acting bug as a young child and

played Cosette in *Les Miserable.* As a young actress, she

had a successful career lasting into her teens doing commercial work and soap operas. More and more, Louise took the role of stage mom, taking Jen to auditions and classes in voice, tap, and ballet. Her parents encouraged her acting dreams.

She landed a prestigious spot in Tisch's Cap 21 program at New York University. Students were selected on their potential talent as a triple threat—not only did they need to be good actors, but they had to excel at singing and dancing. Parents and friends all thought Jennifer's career path was set, but they were wrong.

New York City was full of many other talented young women, and Cap 21 at NYU contained a plethora of ingénue types who snagged the leading roles. After graduation, Jen quickly learned she didn't have the look a director wanted or the type of voice he was after. She would barely start singing before he would shout, "Thank you very much for coming in! Next!"

Although a success in landing jobs as a child and

adolescent actor, she met constant rejection and frustration

as a young adult. No one seemed to want her. She barely

made chorus in a few off-Broadway productions. She

succumbed to the director's couch, but that only led to a few

B roles that never showcased her talent.

After one audition, feeling a tremendous sense of

self-loathing, Jen met a young actor who invited her out for a

cup of coffee. Ryan was tall, handsome, and resembled a

Disney prince. He sensed her discouragement and tried to

be supportive of her abilities, boosting her ego. The

relationship turned serious, and they decided to move in

together, so they set up a small Brooklyn studio apartment.

Life was good at first, and Jen was very happy.

Unfortunately, she still didn't get any roles, but Ryan was

constantly being cast and quickly became a recognized,

sought-after talent. It was hard for Jen to watch his success.

Fights between them intensified, so she decided to end the

relationship.

Ryan wanted to continue their relationship despite Jennifer's insecurities, but she felt it was over. As if things couldn't get any worse, her dad died of a massive heart attack during a business trip two months after she broke up with Ryan.

Jennifer's mom moved back to New Orleans to live with her sister. Louise felt very lonely while married to Robert. Apparently, she knew there was more to his business trips than just business. She hid her suspicions of infidelity from Jen and internalized her anguish and disappointment over her marriage. Louise, longing for the comfort of family, needed to return to her roots.

Louise encouraged Jen to move in with her in New Orleans. She heard the movie business was gaining momentum down there, so maybe a fresh start would help. It couldn't be any worse. She didn't have anything to lose

She felt very depressed when she landed in New

Orleans. In New York, Ryan secured a recurring role on NCIS and only wished her well. Louise enjoyed living with her sister and revisiting her childhood haunts around the city, but Jen didn't share those connection and felt alienated. Surprisingly after the New York City high-pressure lifestyle, Jen acclimated to the slower pace of life in the big easy with the mantra "*Laissez les bon temps rouler*," but something still felt terribly wrong.

One day Jen woke up and realized she embraced the slow-paced life to cover her depression and asked, "What am I doing? This isn't me."

She brushed herself off and said, "No more feeling sorry for myself. It's time to take control and get back to living."

Her first step back to life was to help others who felt worthless and depressed. She became a mental health care volunteer worker. It made a big difference hearing others' despair and realizing she could provide a lifeline for the young girl at the other end of the phone.

She made a big difference in one girl's life. She was sixteen and threatening suicide due to being bullied at school. With Jen's help, the girl got the help she needed.

Eventually, Jennifer felt like she was regaining her old life and self. "No more blues for me!" she exclaimed while enjoying *café au lait* and beignets with a volunteer colleague. Jen found her smile again and sense of purpose. She was even able to share in the joy of Ryan's success and new relationship with a Tony Award-winning actress.

I met Jennifer at a fundraiser for mental health. She was one of the phone volunteers, and I asked to be one of the guest auctioneers. We spoke on break over some stale doughnuts and coffee at the craft table, and something told me we would become fast friends. She was totally honest and vulnerable.

Gradually over drinks and lunches, our friendship grew. Jen hadn't socialized much after returning to New

Orleans. She seemed happy to have a girlfriend to share her deepest thoughts and dreams, and it was clear she was determined to create a meaningful life for herself.

I invited her to a birthday party I was throwing for Terry. During that party and a momentous wine spill, she met Jake Townsend, a forty-two-year-old real-estate magnate from New Orleans. He insisted she have lunch with him, so he could properly apologize for his clumsiness spilling wine over her beautiful dress.

After that luncheon with Jake, they became inseparable. Their wedding took place six months later, and she beamed throughout the ceremony. Louise was so happy that her daughter found someone who respected and loved her. To Louise's delight, Jake wanted kids right away, because he came from a large family.

Jennifer and Jake always appeared like a honeymoon couple, although it was never false or sickening. It was real love mixed with genuine respect for the other. Jennifer couldn't stop smiling and thanking God for Jake's coming into her life.

Two years after the wedding, James was born, a beautiful baby boy who looked just like his father. Jen's life was perfect until the night she got a call from the Lakefront Airport that Jake was involved in a plane crash. He often piloted his private plan to view properties along the Gulf Coast. The weather deteriorated rapidly after his takeoff from Biloxi, Mississippi, and there was a lot of fog around the Lakefront Airport. Jake missed the runway and was killed instantly.

After Jake's death, Jennifer spent her days concentrating on James. She was stronger and more composed than any of us expected. Fortunately, Jake left her very wealthy and secure, especially concerning James' education. She continued to volunteer at the mental health hotline, but her primary goal was to make sure James grew up strong and happy.

He eventually went to Tulane University, then

transferred to NYU. While in New York, he auditioned for

a role on *The Young and Restless.* His career skyrocketed,

and he quickly received offers from Hollywood. Jennifer

made sure he stayed grounded during his rise to fame. She

followed him around on location or made him come home

to New Orleans for some much-needed R&R

I saw a few of James' movies and was impressed by

his strong screen presence. He reminded me a young James

Dean. Jennifer returned to the spotlight through her

talented son, which somehow seemed very right to me.

St Louis Cathedral Jackson Square

This National Historic Landmark sits on 2.5 acres in the center of the Presbytere and Pontalba Buildings. The gardens based are design of 17th-century Place des Vosges in Paris, France. Also an open air art gallery, the site was named for General and future president Andrew Jackson after his victory over the British in the battle of New Orleans in 1815.

CHAPTER FOUR

Adrien

Of all the girls, Adrien was the hardest to get close to and understand, maybe because she was very reserved and kept to herself. She was a green-eyed, chestnut-haired star athlete in school in Hilton Head Island, South Carolina. Her family moved to New Orleans before she graduated from high school.

Her father became a Congressman from New Orleans, which removed him from participating in most of the important events in her young life. Adrien adored her father and missed him terribly.

Upon her graduation from Sacred Heart Academy, she was awarded a women's study scholarship at George

Washington University. Several Ivy League universities accepted her, but she gladly took the offer from GWU to be closer to her dad, hoping they would have more time to spend together if she lived closer to Washington, DC. Unfortunately, that didn't work out.

While in college, she received an internship on Capitol Hill and met a young Senator from Virginia named Shepherd Collins. He was struck by her good looks and enthusiastic work ethic, while she was swept off her feet by his stately stature and handsome face. He resembled a young John F. Kennedy.

Although there was ten years' difference in their ages, Adrien didn't think that was significant. Their relationship progressed quickly. He squired her around town, took her to state dinners at the White House, and involved her in discussions about his proposed legislation. She soon found herself flying to Charlottesville to meet his parents, who were old-Virginia aristocracy and extremely wealthy. Shepherd, nicknamed "Shep," attended the University of Virginia and was part of the privileged horse set.

Shep's love of horses took him all over the country to compete in equestrian events. His parents supported that love and invested in thoroughbreds, with two of their three-year-olds running in the Kentucky Derby. During his years in Charlottesville, Shep met another horse lover named Anna, a divorced woman ten years his senior. She and Shep became inseparable on the horse circuit, charity events, and even during his run for Congress. Anna stayed behind the curtain during his campaign, but she was with him every night. Shep's parents didn't approve of the relationship and assumed it ended after his election and move to Washington, DC.

Shep's parents instantly liked Adrien. She was educated, lovely, and came from good stock, as if she were a young thoroughbred. She would be the perfect "arm ornament" for a rising political star. They put a lot of pressure on Shep to take his relationship with her to the next step.

Wanting to appease them and remain in their good favor, he complied. In whirlwind fashion, Shep and Adrien eloped to Las Vegas during a Congressional recess to get married, although it wasn't the wedding she dreamed of having. The Little Chapel in Las Vegas, complete with plastic flowers and canned organ music, served its purpose. She became Mrs. Shepherd Collins and was very happy. Her future looked bright and filled with wonderful possibilities.

Upon returning to Washington, Adrien threw herself into redecorating their Georgetown brownstone and creating a home. She wanted to be an asset to Shep in every possible way, including hosting teas for other Congressional wives and working at charity events. She was so busy trying to create the perfect life, she didn't seem to realize Shep was almost never home. She thought he was hard at work drafting an environmental bill and making himself a political asset to his party.

Unfortunately, the environmental bill turned out to be nights spent with Anna. Many months later, a good friend told Adrien she saw Shep and Anna arm-in-arm in the lobby of the Mayflower Hotel. Adrien was devastated. Another important man in her life, like her father, had abandoned her.

As soon as possible, she divorced Shep. His parents made sure the divorce was amicable, and Adrien was well-compensated. She wanted nothing more to do with politics, Washington, or Shep, so she packed her bags and headed back to New Orleans to clear her head and figure out her next move.

She stayed with her aunt, because her parents thought she made a huge mistake divorcing someone who might potentially become the next President.

"Adrien, you just need to overlook this little dalliance and think of the bigger picture," her father said emphatically. "For goodness' sake, grow up!"

Later, Adrien told her aunt, "So much for parental support."

I met Adrien at a friend's dinner party. We didn't become instant fast friends, but we shared a love for English literature and '80s oldies music. We talked about her move back to New Orleans and recovery from Shep. She accepted a teaching position in literature at Louise S. McGehee's School, a private girl's school in the Garden District founded in 1912. The history and look of the school appealed to her romanticism and Jane Eyre mentality. She came to adore the girls, and they loved her. She had a knack for bringing literature alive for her pupils. She encouraged them to write their own stories and poems.

"Write from your hearts," she said.

Adrien had some of her poetry published in *Stone*

Soup. A few of her students went on to become creative writing teachers. One became a famous children's book author, winning the prestigious Newberry Award.

I thought it would be good for Adrien to meet the girls, so I invited her to our holiday luncheon. She took a personal, day off from McGehee's to attend and was easily accepted into the group, becoming a regular. I never knew how she managed to take a personal day off from work each month to attend our lunches, but no one seemed upset by it.

"I thought teachers had a hard time missing school," I often remarked.

Unlike her usual reserved persona, Adrien at the lunches became pretty rowdy and wasn't one to hold back on martinis and spout off about how the important men in her life hurt her. Those lunches, very therapeutic in her healing process, helped distance her from Shep.

At least she was emerging from the shadows of disappointment. Her anger was slowly replaced by acceptance and a "let's move on with life" attitude.

As far as I knew, Adrien never had another relationship with any eligible New Orleans bachelor. Her alimony from Shep kept her very comfortable, and there was a rumor she was living with a female art professor named Cynthia who taught at Newcomb College. They fell deeply in love, having many things in common, and the relationship was strong for a few years.

None of the girls in the group commented, challenged, or chastised Adrien over the news. After all, wasn't the goal to be happy?

However one reached nirvana, it was fine with me as long as she didn't cause harm along the way. Adrien slowly distanced herself from me and the girls. Maybe she thought we were too narrow-minded to handle her relationship with Cynthia. She always sent the usual Christmas and birthday cards to each of us, but that was the extent of our communication.

It would be good to see her again and catch up. I was frankly surprised that she accepted the luncheon invitation with such enthusiasm.

Cemeteries

A popular attraction are the above ground crypts and tombs with graves dating to the 1700's. Their eerie structures are likened unto 'Cities of the Dead'. Visitors may hear the rough "caw" and "kraa" of crows and ravens as the sinister black birds keep watch over the departed.

CHAPTER FIVE

Courtney

Courtney Breaux came from a poor family living in the small town of Donaldsonville, Louisiana. Her parents barely graduated from high school. Dad worked on the oil rigs, and her mother took care of their six children.

From a young age, Courtney had to help with chores and take care of the younger kids. Her dad was often laid off from work, which meant she had to take odd jobs to supplement the family income. Working made her miss school, which was hard on her, because it was the only place she felt free and happy. The other students complained about their homework, but not Courtney. She was eager to graduate high school and attend college. Unfortunately, she had little hope of that.

Most of her girlfriends married and were pregnant by seventeen. Courtney longed for something more but didn't see a way out. She was twenty-two and worked at a local seafood restaurant, still maintaining her hope of a better life, as she took a few online college courses.

She was a voracious reader. Every chance she got, she went to the local library and absorbed herself in English novels, history books, and world events. Her friends thought she was odd and needed to have a baby on her hip. Her family agreed and thought she should give up on her pipedreams.

"No good can come from thinking you can be better than you are and the way God made you," her mother told her.

Courtney believed God wanted her to have the best

life she could achieve.

A young entrepreneur named Seth Banyan came to town with his sights set on building a steel mill outside Donaldsonville. The Louisiana legislature passed some enticing tax breaks for such an endeavor.

He was schooled back East, the son of a Carnegie Mellon industrialist with assets that included copper mines and oil wells in Texas and throughout the Gulf of Mexico. He was six-feet tall and extremely good looking at his thirty years.

He walked into Courtney's restaurant with three of his management team members hungry for some good Southern fried chicken and cold beer. He sat at Courtney's table, and her beautiful dark eyes met his over the menu.

By the time the meal ended, he was hooked and asked her out. He suggested they go to dinner at Arnaud's Restaurant in New Orleans on Saturday, flying her there in his private plane. She politely declined, because she had nothing to wear and felt uncomfortable.

The next day, twelve dresses from Saks were delivered to her home, along with a seamstress to make any necessary alterations. A variety of shoes, bags, and jewelry to accessorize her chosen outfit were also included. Courtney was persuaded to accept Seth's invitation.

The date with Seth could have been taken straight out of *Pretty Woman.* Courtney was wined and dined. She never experienced such a Cinderella moment, and four waiters catered to their every need.

After dinner, Seth took her to the Carousel Bar at the Monteleone Hotel for champagne. She expected him to ask for sex in return, but he took her back to the Lakefront Airport in his limo, where they boarded the plane at midnight and flew back to Donaldsonville.

They were married in Paris, France. Seth was a pure romantic in everything he did for Courtney.

They put down roots in North Dallas. Their home,

situated on half an acre of enviable real estate, was a show-

stopper filled with beautiful furnishings and art.

Architectural Digest featured the estate in a spread about

fabulous homes belonging to Texas' young social elite. Most

charities used the home for philanthropic events.

Seth and Courtney quickly became very popular and

were invited to all the big parties. Her lack of formal

education didn't prevent her from rising to the top of the

Dallas social set, raising millions for local causes.

After three years of marriage, Courtney gave birth to

adorable fraternal twins named Amanda and Benjamin.

They brought joy to both parents, and they were terribly

spoiled. Seth had a playground and petting stable built on

the property. The children had walk-in closets to store all

their designer outfits. Nothing was too expensive when it

came to those kids.

Seth surprised Courtney each month marking the

day of their first date in New Orleans with an extravagant

bauble or present.

There's nothing too extravagant for my girl, he
always wrote on the gift card. Thank you *for my children
and for completing my life.*

Terry and I met Courtney at a Dallas fundraisers
given at her home. Courtney was the chairwoman of the
event. Initially, Terry and I cringed at the thought of
attending the affair, because we assumed it would be a
boring evening, but we wanted to see the estate we read
about in *Architectural Digest.*

It was hard to turn down an opportunity to raise
money for childhood cancer research. Courtney came to
our table to thank us for attending, since we represented the
$2,500 donor level. She pulled up a chair and started
talking to Terry.

She was grounded and funny, and I knew
immediately she'd fit in with the other girls, so I invited her
to my next luncheon.

After that, she became a regular part of the group, entertaining us with tales of life on the bayou and anecdotes from her Southern roots while sipping Maker's Mark over ice.

Five years after her marriage to Seth, I received a hysterical call from Courtney at 3:00 AM. She said Seth was arrested for murdering a company executive. He hired a hit man at the request of the executive's wife with whom Seth was having an affair. He was also accused of embezzling millions of company dollars.

"What?" I asked in disbelief.

Seth was convicted and sentence to life imprisonment. At first, Courtney didn't divorce him, but by the time all the lawsuits were settled, she and the children were almost bankrupt.

"How could Seth do this to me?" she asked over the phone.

A divorce quickly followed.

Seth's mother, Leona, loved Courtney as if she were her own daughter. Courtney helped Leona through the ordeal and shielded her from the hateful press coverage and public opinion.

Since Leona came from old family wealth, she provided Courtney and her children enough money to start over and be comfortable.

"What good is money if it can't help you at this point in your life?" Leona asked. "I'm comfortable enough and don't need much."

Leona hugged her, and Courtney realized the woman gave her more motherly love and support than her own family.

Courtney took the kids and moved to New Orleans. The Southern lifestyle always appealed to her, and New Orleans was "a small town with a city atmosphere."

The change was good for all of them. She invited Leona to join them, but the stress took its toll on Leona's health, and she passed soon after she moved to New Orleans. Courtney devoted herself to raising her children and providing them the best-possible education.

Under the circumstances, the children fared well. Eventually, Amanda attended Newcomb College. After graduation, she went on to study fashion in France. Benjamin majored in business at Tulane University, and then he attended the prestigious London School of Business and Finance.

The last time I heard anything about Courtney, she bought a small café on Annunciation Street to serve the lunch crowd, but not quite our crowd. She served oyster and shrimp poor boys and muffulettas and gumbo to the local dock workers.

A fifty-year-old burly worker named Joe Boudreaux became a regular customer. She grew up in Donaldsonville and knew Courtney in high school. They hadn't socialized in school, having very different circles of friends. He finally mustered the courage to ask her on a date.

That one date became the first of many. Although
they never married, they enjoyed each other's company.
People reported she seemed happy. Courtney had returned
home to her country roots.

Streetcar

One must remember that in New Orleans these are streetcars and not trollies. Dating back to 1835, with the St. Charles Avenue line there are now four additional lines. They are Avenue Line, the Riverfront Line, the Canal Street Line, and the Loyola Avenue Line and Rampart/St. Claude Line.

CHAPTER SIX

Kathy

I met Kathy the first day of our medical internship. We were a special class of only six female interns. Since we were something of an oddity, we banded together. The girls were from all over, but Kathy, a redheaded, green-eyed beauty, grew up in the Irish Channel in New Orleans. She was the first in her family to go to college and earn a graduate degree. We had a lot in common and talked about everything from guzzling green beer at Parasol's Bar on St. Patrick's Day to loving bike rides through Audubon Park. Like me, she was goal-oriented and very driven to get accepted into medical school, foregoing any personal relationships along the way.

Kathy wanted to become a pulmonary specialist. She experienced a family member's death from lung cancer and wanted to do research to find a cure. The experience of her uncle's death took a toll on the entire family. Shortly after the death, Kathy's mom became extremely depressed and committed suicide. Her mother suffered from manic depression and couldn't afford the cost of therapy or medication, partly because she was too proud to ask for financial help.

Kathy became a strong advocate of affordable medical care, including mental health benefits, and she lobbied anyone who would listen. She wrote letters to state and national leaders pleading for help for those who couldn't afford medications or medical care. Kathy even proposed ideas for legislation and how affordable health care could be structured and financed.

Although our internship was tough, we managed to get together over midnight coffee in the doctors' lounge. On our days off, we often did laundry at one of the girl's apartments and gossiped over beer and pizza while watching old movies on TV. We spoke of our work, lack of sleep, and the future. There were social occasions in which the senior medical staff sponsored holiday parties, complete with a band and open bar. Usually, one or more of us had to ward off the advances of a staff member and ended up leaving early.

The young male interns were all married, with wives who worked to put them through medical school. Those very protective women hovered over their men, refusing to let them socialize with our group.

After internship, Kathy and I went on to residencies in New Orleans. Post residency, Kathy joined a successful pulmonary practice and continued her advocacy fight for affordable medical care. She traveled to Washington, DC, several times to demonstrate or talk to lawmakers. She even appeared before the House Health and Welfare Committee to testify. She was passionate and brilliant speaker. I told her she needed to run for Congress, but she simply said, "No, thanks. I'll continue to battle in the trenches."

Over the years, I introduced her to the girls' lunch group, and she became regular. The girls loved her immediately. Terry and Kathy became fast friends, partly due to their shared love of scientific research. I hated organic chemistry in school, but they loved talking about molecular structures and peptides as if they were discussing *Fashion Week*. Terry was always looking for the next, best anti-aging cream. Kathy and Terry talked for hours about possible study trials. Terry wanted Kathy to join her company and head the research and development unit, but Kathy politely declined.

When I married, Kathy was one of my bridesmaids. I tried to be a matchmaker for her, but all attempts were rebuffed. She was absorbed by her practice and advocacy efforts. Kathy said she didn't need marriage to fulfill her life. She had male friends and went on dinner dates, which was good enough. She admitted to wanting a child and was considering adoption. She talked about going to Africa to adopt and contacted a legal specialist who could help her maneuver through the laborious process.

One day in the hospital hallway, Grace, one of Kathy's partners, rushed up to me noticeably shaken and grabbed my arm. I assumed one of her dementia patients grabbed her butt or breast.

"Kathy's sick," she said.

"What do you mean?" I thought she just had a cold or the flu.

Kathy had been spitting up blood for weeks and hadn't told anyone. During hospital rounds, Kathy's serious coughing attack forced her to be examined by a fellow physician.

The chest X-ray was undeniable. A large tumor occupied her left lower lung lobe. A series of blood tests, CT scans, and oncology consultations followed. The cancer metastasized to her liver, brain, and bone. Three months later, Kathy was dead.

I began questioning everything. What was her life for? Why had it been extinguished at such a young age? She gave everything to becoming a physician and advocating for those less fortunate. She was close to adopting a six-year-old Ethiopian girl whose life would have been radically changed. Now Kathy was gone, and I struggled to find a reason.

It took me awhile to realize I was going through the normal stages of grief. People who are smart often consider themselves immune to the common thoughts and experiences of others. I felt I should have been able to reason and solve my problem. I'd been solving problems my entire adult life, but I couldn't reason my way out of that one.

It took me a long, hard time to deal with Kathy's death. I suffered from insomnia, went through many bottles of vodka, and started stupid fights with my husband. My work suffered. I misdiagnosed a problem that almost cost one patient's life, because I was consumed with self-pity and doubt.

I finally told myself, "I'm as human as the next person. I need time to grieve."

Kathy was a wonderful young woman whose mission was to be an outstanding physician helping those less fortunate. She should have had a long life to accomplish her dreams, but life isn't always fair.

At her funeral, I thought, *She must be looking down at us, smiling to see how many of her patients attended to show their love for her. I doubt I'd get four to come to mine.*

I realized Kathy gave me a valuable gift of genuine

friendship and love. Through our all-too-brief relationship,

I learned about generosity of spirit and caring for others. I

became a better person for having known her.

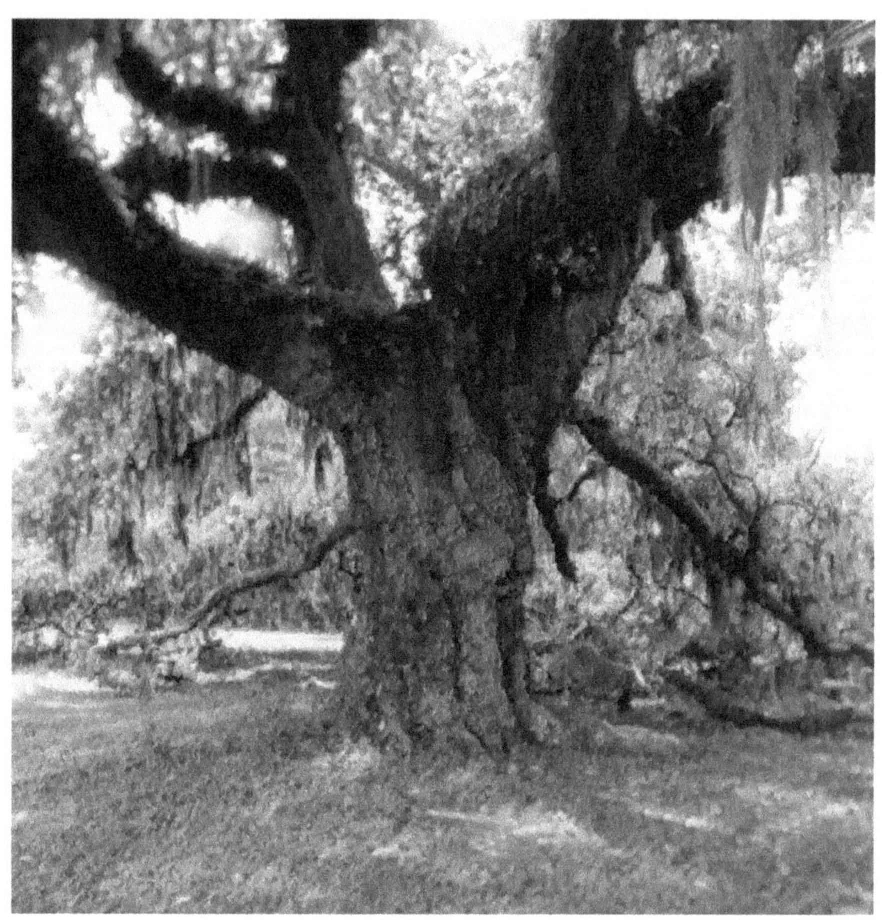

Dueling Oaks

In the 18th and 19th centuries many squabbles and insults were settled on the greens where now sits City Park. Once a pair, the Dueling Oaks along with crowds of more than a hundred witnessed the clash of swords and pistols fought to redress grievances. Reports say as many as a dozen duels were fought on any given day and the combatants included men and women. Only one of the oak survives to this day.

CHAPTER SEVEN

Post-Kathy

The first luncheon after Kathy's death was my

responsibility. I wanted to cancel, but we needed a chance

to reconnect and have some fun.

I looked for a restaurant that would serve comfort

food in a family atmosphere and found Irene's on Bienville

Street in the French Quarter. There were photos on the

wall of many of us. Irene always made her customers feel

like family. Her food and drink filled us with a sense of

home and belonging. I loved the crusty bruschetta loaded

with ripe tomatoes. The menu included wonderful mussels

with linguini, clams casino, and fabulous ossobuco. One of

my favorite dishes was spaghetti and meatballs, an homage to

Irene's Italian father.

We had the entire rear section of the dining room. Since it was Halloween, I decorated the table with pumpkins and black and orange candles. Down the center of the table was a black sequined table runner adorned with cobwebs and plastic spiders. A plastic witch's hat sat on each chair, tied to the back with an orange satin bow. Candy corn confetti was sprinkled around each place setting, consisting of orange plates and black wine goblets. Sitting on each plate was a wrapped gift box containing orange, crystal pumpkin earrings as a party favor for each guest. In the center of the table was a boiling caldron filled with dry ice. It looked *fabulosa*!

I always loved Halloween. The orange and black decorations and carved pumpkins set aglow with candles made me smile. When I was a little girl, Mom made Halloween special by decorating the house inside and out. We had a noisy witch's howl door knocker, cobwebs over the tree branches, and a Halloween tree decorated with sequined black bats, purple witches, and orange pumpkins. I loved dress up for trick or treat as a child. Later in life, I wore a costume when I handed out candy to the neighborhood kids in New Orleans.

Halloween was a big deal at the homes along St. Charles Avenue, with everyone trying to outdo each other with cemetery headstones in the front yards and giant spiders hanging from the magnolia trees. The other big draw about Halloween was that it usually heralded a change in the weather. We finally reached the time of year when the days started to get cooler, dropping to eighty degrees instead of ninety.

First to arrive was Terry, wearing an orange feather boa draped over a black sequined sheath dress embellished with orange crystals. Her hair was done up in a French twist with rhinestone spiders along the edge. Her black Louboutin shoes and Hermes bag completed her outfit.

Heads turned, as they always did, when she entered the room.

"Hey, there, Girlfriend," she said. "Where's my whiskey sour?"

"It's on its way, complete with plastic spider decoration."

She looked fit and well. As she sipped her cocktail, she said her national business continued to flourish. She was considering taking Flawless, Inc. global.

Just as I was about to ask for details, Jennifer and Adrien arrived. Jennifer wore a satin black- and white-striped pantsuit that hugged her size-four figure. Adrien flaunted an orange mini with black leather top and jacket adorned with a giant Swarovski spider. Last to arrive was Courtney in a black lace dress replete with orange applique pumpkins. I knew it wasn't something she bought at Saks. She loved having clothing custom made for special occasions.

All the outfits were over the top.

"Well, aren't we all the pretty pumpkins?" I asked, feeling like we were there to rekindle good times.

My first impression evaporated quickly. Soon after multiple Bloody Marys, whiskey sours, and Sazeracs, the first shot was fired when Terry accused Courtney of sitting around and feeling sorry for herself.

"Why don't you look for productive work or pursue some adult courses toward a college degree?" Terry asked. "You can't wait for life to hand you success. You have to work for it." Her third whiskey sour splashed on the table when she set it down.

Courtney tried to tell Terry she was perfectly happy, visiting Amanda and Benjamin when she could and staying home. "I enjoy gardening and reading. My life is full."

"You aren't eighty years old," Terry shot back.

Suddenly, Jennifer said, "Just shut your trap, Terry, and leave her alone."

As adolescent as it sounded, a bruschetta loaded with tomatoes sailed through the air and landed in Jennifer's lap. I thought I saw a Louboutin shoe hurled toward Courtney.

These compulsive, violent exchanges weren't our norm. Where was the laughter and bawdy camaraderie? What happened to trigger such an outburst?

Much later that night, after the failed luncheon, I realized Kathy's absence was the key. The girls were angry that she died. Perhaps their grieving process, like mine, was delayed. We'd lost someone dear to us, almost a sister. Kathy helped complete the group. Our intimate circle had a hole in it, and we didn't know how to compensate for the loss.

Thankfully, we recovered in time for the next luncheon given by Terry at Thanksgiving. The girls were all smiles and laughter as if there was no drama at the previous meeting. We never mentioned Kathy again. Perhaps that was a defense against sadness dominating our mood and thoughts.

After all, we were the invincible female movers and shakers in the "city that care forgot." We had it made. Sadness wasn't part of the successful equation of our lives. We believed we were immune to any semblance of doom and gloom.

That was our last luncheon. It wasn't the way I wanted to remember the end of our girls' lunches.

Blue and White Street Tiles

Installed at the intersection of streets in 1870's, the iconic blue and white tiles marked the names at a time when pedestrian traffic was more common. So remember to look down at intersections before looking left and right.

CHAPTER EIGHT

The Lunch

"The gang's all here," I exclaimed, as I reached the table.

Immediately, I started hugging and air-kissing each of them.

"You look fabulous, Dear," Terry said. "How much weight have you lost?"

Mission accomplished! I thought. "Oh, about fifteen pounds with the help of a trainer, nutritionist, and a private chef." I laughed. "I think each lost pound cost me about five hundred dollars."

I settled into my spot beside Courtney, as two waiters arrived to take our drink orders. I immediately felt a sense of home and belonging. A jazz trio started playing, *Do You*

I felt Satchmo's spirit in the room.

"Let's order a bottle of Cristal champagne to celebrate!" Terry said.

"Absolutely," Jennifer said. "It's been twenty-five years since we were together."

As I looked at the others, I saw time had left its mark in tiny lines on each face. They maintained their looks with Botox, facial peels, and every Retinol cream on the market, but some lines didn't go away.

Terry was the first to volunteer, "For the next luncheon, I'll have a new face. I'm scheduled for a facelift in two weeks."

I tried to remember how many procedures that made but lost count. Her remark started a discussion about plastic surgery that continued as the iced champagne arrived. As the bottle was popped and poured, I thought, *And they're off.*

The Oysters Rockefeller was as yummy as I remembered. Our waiter delivered the Creole tomatoes and buffalo mozzarella, fried calamari, shrimp remoulade, and hot French bread. As I consumed appetizers and sipped champagne, the old sound of giggles and laughter erupted around the table. It felt good to look around and see the smiles and hear the banter again. After twenty-five years, the group reacted as if time hadn't moved a bit. I loved the feeling I experienced at the luncheons when we were young and fearless. I always felt my life was still ahead of me, with no thought of mortality or mundane worries. Twenty-five years earlier, each of us was oblivious to the challenges we would someday confront and the concessions we would have to make. Youth was great, and we felt invincible.

Now I was in my fifties, and reality reared its head to erase those easy feeling of immortality. I wasn't sure if I would disclose my medical condition to the others. Why ruin the mood?

"Who knows?" my husband asked. "You may go into remission any day."

I was diagnosed with multiple sclerosis a month earlier. I knew something was wrong when I began to lose vision in my left eye and had ptosis of the left upper eyelid, a condition where drooping of the eyelid was a key sign of neurological diseases like MS and myasthenia gravis. Amazingly, I was pretty calm about the diagnosis.

"We can't assume anything nor predict the course of the disease," my husband told me, trying to remain positive, but I knew he was thinking that our active lifestyle in Colorado would end.

When the doctor becomes the patient, a disconnect occurs. Everything one learned either went out the window or one began to second-guess every decision, because one knew too much. I did the latter. I was a perfect example of the belief that doctors didn't make very good patients.

"Another bottle of Cristal," Terry told the waiter.

We were awaiting our amazing entrées, which ranged from shrimp etouffee and soft-shelled crab to filet mignon and lobster. My mouth was watering. I loved New Orleans food.

There was a famous local saying: "We live to eat, not eat to live."

Maybe that was why Louisiana had one of the highest rates of stroke and heart disease in the country.

That day wasn't about health but indulging in all things delicious and fun. Laughter and joy spilled over into the room. Heads turned our way. Unbelievably, a gray-haired gentleman in a pin-striped suit came over to us and said, "I remember you ladies." He winked at me, as he walked away.

It was time for dessert, coffee, and Grand Marnier. As I started digging into the baked Alaska, Courtney said, "It's time to share and bring everyone up to speed. I'll go first. I met a wonderful man named Bob who works

offshore on the oil rigs. I had been seeing a man named

Joe, but he lied about being married. His wife came to my

café one day to tell me Joe was married, with six kids and

four grandchildren.

"I parted ways with Joe. When I went home to

Donaldsonville to attend the local crayfish festival, I met

Bob. Even though he was born and raised in

Donaldsonville, we never met.

"He said he remembered me from the old days

when I worked at the seafood restaurant. He approaches

each day as a gift and makes me feel so good." She beamed.

"Bob sounds like a keeper to me," I said.

Apparently, all wasn't as good from Courtney's

children's standpoint concerning Bob. Benjamin and

Amanda were adamant that he was the wrong partner for

her. They were skeptical of his intentions and viewed him as

a gold-digger.

Courtney said a nasty legal fight developed between her and the kids, who wanted to protect their inheritance, so she said they could have it all. She was perfectly happy to move back to Donaldsonville and live on Bob's salary.

It was funny. She always wanted to escape the small-town life but was suddenly willing to move back into that peaceful, slow pace. There was something symmetrical and right about her plans. Money never held the save revered status for her that it did for most of us.

I was happy for her and hoped the children would rally around her. She planned to move in with Bob within a month, and they would marry soon after.

"You're all invited," she said. "It won't be a Fairmont catered affair, but we'll have plenty of crayfish and beer."

"OK," Adrien said. "I'll go next. Cynthia and I have decided to move to Paris. I want to absorb myself in another culture. She'll paint, and we'll both travel, drink wine, and enjoy the rest of our days. I have stage-four breast cancer and have used up my options. Don't weep or gasp. I'm reconciled with my future."

Stunned, we fell silent.

"We want only what is best for you," I said at last, "and whatever makes you happy. We love you. We'll just have to plan lunch in Paris."

There were a few uncomfortable giggles at my comment.

"This lunch has meant a lot to me," Adrien said. "I find comfort in knowing that through the years, I could depend on all of you to be supportive and not judgmental of whatever I did. I love you guys."

That started most of us crying. We each stood and hugged her as if for the last time. After she distanced herself from us in recent years, I never anticipated hearing her be so grateful about our relationships. The openness and vulnerability she exhibited were a wonderful surprise.

Were these truthful revelations an indication that we were getting older? Perhaps, but I felt that we'd all lost our feelings of youthful immortality and grown into calm, mature admissions of where each of us was in life. We were confronting our future while also expressing how important relationships with each other had been on our journey. We needed to take stock and express our love for one another.

I liked the vulnerability, but I also felt saddened. We were strong women who controlled our future, but life was telling us something different. It sounded like something from a Hallmark card, but life passed in a blink. I longed for the carefree spirit of those thirty-year-old women, but I was simultaneously proud of the women seated before me.

"I'm next," Jennifer said. "After Jake's death, I concentrated on raising James and not much more. He developed into a loving young man who deeply appreciates his mother. He's a successful actor living in New York City,

and he recently met an actress in a play. They have a little
girl named Maisie.”

Jennifer clearly adored her grandchild and spent
most of her time flying back and forth to New York. On
one such visit, she had lunch with an old agent friend who
told her about a part in an upcoming play. Jennifer was
interested, but she hadn’t done any auditions, let alone
acting, in years.

“What have you got to lose?” her agent friend asked.
“It’s a perfect part for you, about a woman who lost her
husband at a young age and suddenly had to cope with
supporting herself and her son.”

After lunch, the agent arranged for Jen to meet the
director, who thought she was perfect for the part.

“I finally had the right look,” Jennifer joked. “I got
the part, and we start rehearsals soon in New York City.
Opening night on Broadway will be in six weeks.”

Although her theatrical dreams took a forty-year

hiatus, they came to fruition.

"I guess it's true that you should never stop dreaming," she said.

We howled with excitement and applause, raising our glasses in a toast.

"*Salut,* Jennifer!" I said. "We'll be there on opening night."

Suddenly, I felt them turn their attention to me. I didn't want to discuss having MS, but everyone else had been so honest, that I cleared my throat and sipped my cognac before saying, "I was recently diagnosed with MS."

Questions came immediately.

"How bad is it?"

"Are you on any treatment?"

"What does your husband think?"

"Are you depressed?"

Why such a grilling? I wondered. Maybe it helps them feel better about their own situations. "All I'll say is that the prognosis is unknown at this time. I'm hoping for the best. Let's hug it out and enjoy this time with each other."

My remarks had the same effect as having all our mothers step into the room and stop us from spiraling out of control.

Suddenly, Terry sang the first line of *Do You Know What It Means to Miss New Orleans?* All the others chimed in.

Terry was the last to share. "My business has become extremely lucrative and is providing me with a luxurious lifestyle. My company has exploded on the national and international fronts."

"You've made it!" someone shouted.

"Yeah, that's great. I invented anti-wrinkle creams. So what? I've been looking for a way to effect real change and leave a legacy. After thinking long and hard, I came up with a charity idea that can truly change lives.

"I established an organization to address the needs of homeless women and their kids. I call it Family Outreach. We take single moms off the streets, give them a modest home, and educate them with a skill to work in one of my offices. I initiated flexible scheduling for the women and provide childcare while they're at work.

"It's been a huge success. So far, Family Outreach has gotten 150 women and their children off the streets. Now don't get all sloppy on me, but perhaps this initiative fills the hole left by not having children with Stan."

Who would have thought that the gal jet-setting around the world in private jets, the queen of one-line zingers and putting people in their place, would turn out to be so charitable to those who lived on the fringe of society?

Our luncheon was fast approaching the fourth hour, with four bottles of champagne consumed along with numerous individual drinks. The dining room was empty except for us.

Suddenly, the room became very quiet.

"The party's over, Girls," Terry said. "It's time to go."

As we left the Sazerac Room, I looked back and smiled. We walked arm-in-arm through the hotel lobby. Outside, sunlight streamed down on the entrance steps.

"Time for a photo!" I shouted.

We took the same photo twenty-five years earlier. Each of us alternately took a position on each side of the center rail. No one needed to be told where to stand. It was in our DNA.

The valet counted down, snapping the photo in each of our phones or cameras. I had the feeling Kathy stood at the top of the stairs, smiling down on us.

ABOUT THE BOOK

Girl's Lunch is a story about six vibrant, talented women who would meet once a month for a celebratory lunch at some of New Orleans' famous restaurants. The lunches were a chance to laugh, gossip, and savor the cuisine of New Orleans. The girls continued their dining events for several decades sharing their accomplishments, joys, sorrows, marriages, children and desires. As the years passed, the lunches eventually disappeared. Now, after twenty-five years, the girls were coming together for one more lunch. A type of unique reunion at the Fairmont Hotel's Sazerac Restaurant. What has everyone been doing and what has happened in the lives of these women who were going to take on the world and make their mark? The flavors of the food, uniqueness of the city and vibrant women make this tantalizing story a great beach or airplane read.

ABOUT THE AUTHOR

Monica L Monica was born at Touro Infirmary in New Orleans while her dad was attending Tulane University. After living mostly in the South, she returned to Tulane University and graduated cum laude. She then went on to receive an MD, PhD from Louisiana State Medical School. Later in life, she received an MHA from Tulane University. She completed an Ophthalmology Residency and practiced in the New Orleans area for over 25 years. Dr. Monica was elected to both national and state leadership positions in Ophthalmology. She ran for Congress in 1999 during which, sadly, her father passed away.

Monica wrote two children's books, "Freckles Goes to Grand Cayman" and "Freckles Goes to Washington D.C." The former book was an homage to the many trips she had taken to Grand Cayman with her family and parents.

Monica still resides in the New Orleans area with her physician husband, Daniel Long. She has two daughters, Lisa, who works in film, and Danielle, who is a producer at Williamstown Theatre Festival.

New Orleans is a fun-loving city filled with people who enjoy eating and celebrating. Over the years, Monica became enamored with the "ladies who lunch" and decided to capture the flavor.

ABOUT THE ILLUSTRATOR

Author/Illustrator Michael Verrett was born in St. Mary Parish in in south central Louisiana a block away from fields of swaying green sugar cane and just down the road from the unhurried Bayou Teche.

He and the author previous collaborated on the children's picture book, Emeline Meets Lavender the Mermaid, written by Monica L. Monica and her granddaughter Emeline Monica King.

An author and illustrator, he has written/illustrated and contributed art to over 110 books. By his estimate he had created over 1200 illustrations. His art began with crayons on the bedroom wall at age 4. He studied art at Louisiana State University, Scottsdale Art Institute, and the FBI academy.

 A retired homicide detective/police sketch artist he completed the FBI's school of fascial forensic artist which is limited to 20 students from around the world and once a year. His clearance rate for murderers is the highest in the department's history. On the subject of homicide and law he has lectured at Southern University, Louisiana State University, Southeaster Louisiana University and for the U S Attorney's Office on homicide procedures and in regional training centers.

In addition, he has held many other colorful careers to include:

Gifted Arts Teacher for the West Baton Rouge Parish School System.

Emergency Manager and Logistics Chief for the Governor's Office of Homeland Security. Hired in the aftermath of Hurricane Katrina as the Logistics Chief, he created the state's emergency response plan for critical emergency supplies and transportation nexus so that the state could pre-stage supplies prior to disasters as well as well deliver sufficient food, water, and other essentials in future events. Do to the state's resounding success in other disasters, FEMA had him provide instructional lectures to other state's on the subject. He as responded to some of the nation's largest disasters providing over one million meals a day and two million bottles of water during Hurricane Gustav and Ike, provided material and expertise in the aftermath of the BP Oil spill, and was sent to New York to assist the city for Superstorm Sandy.

He also created the Get a Fame Plan coloring book for the Governor that provided instruction for emergency preparedness that were made available for every elementary student in the state.

LT. Colonel U S Army. Michael served over 30 years of active duty and reserves. As an officer, he wore a number of hats from Infantry, Fire Team Support, Military Intelligence, an instructor at the Army's Command & General Staff College, and a staff officer stationed with 3rd Army during the war (2004-2005) where he oversaw the recovery of antiquities for the people of Iraq as well as over $100M worth of misplaced/lost military equipment.

An awardee of the Bronze Star, he travels had an office at the pentagon, but an address in Kuwait where he travels to several around the region to include Africa as part of his duties. While at 3rd Army he produced an illustrated book on convoy procedures for distribution to civilian drivers who could not comprehend English or Arabic or were illiterate.

He is the past-president of the Livingston Parish Arts Council, past-president of Spotlight Theater, A member of the Society of Children's Book Writers and Illustrators, A board member of Creative Minds Writers of Ponchatoula, LA, and a former member of the LSU Operetta.

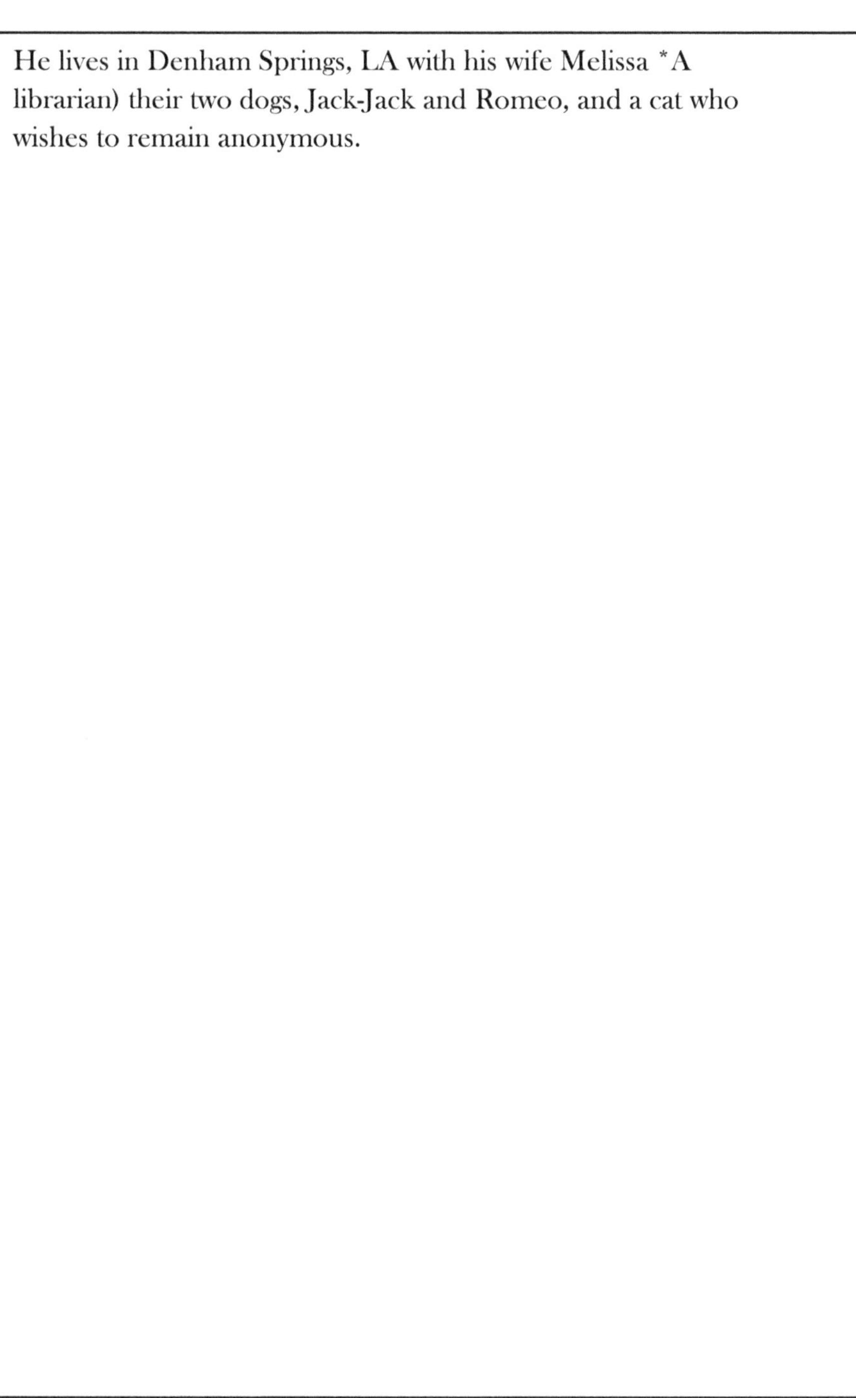

He lives in Denham Springs, LA with his wife Melissa *A librarian) their two dogs, Jack-Jack and Romeo, and a cat who wishes to remain anonymous.